Ramadan

Time for Sharing

It is Ramadan.

When it is Ramadan,

our family will be together.

When it is Ramadan,
I will go to the **mosque**
and **pray**.

7

When it is Ramadan,

I will say thank you.

I will say thank you

for my family.

I will say thank you

for my food.

I will say thank you

for my friends.

When it is Ramadan,
I will read to my dad.

When it is Ramadan,
we will be happy.

Glossary

mosque

pray